NEW JOB NEW YOU

How to write a job application that will get you noticed

Gwyneth Letherbarrow MBA

The information you'll find in this book is to educate you. We make no promise or guarantee of income or earnings.

Please email gwyneth@feelgoodcoachingandconsulting.com if you would like to know more.

ISBN-13: 978-1983890062
ISBN-10: 1983890065

To new beginnings, bold decisions, and brighter futures.

CONTENTS

FOREWORD

Back in late 2012, I was running a CV writing and interview skills workshop when one participant confided in me that he was deeply worried about his future. His company was downsizing, and because several people were doing the same role, he would have to reapply for his own job.

He was convinced he wouldn't be successful. "My colleague gets on better with the boss," he said. Despite his concerns, he worked hard throughout the workshop, yet I could tell he still had a lot of inner questions to wrestle with.

Around six months later, I returned to the same company to run more workshops. One day, I received a message: someone wanted to speak to me. When I turned to greet him, I didn't immediately recognise the confident, smiling face.

"I got the job," he said. "Thank you for changing my life."

I was stunned—and overjoyed. This was the same young man who had once seemed so close to giving up. He explained that he'd taken everything from the workshop on board and had worked hard at rebranding himself.

But the truth is, I didn't change his life, **he** did. He gained clarity on where he wanted to be and then took the steps to get there. That's the key. Especially now, more than ever, you need to be clear about what you're aiming for. Otherwise, you risk wasting time and energy on applications that don't align with your goals or values.

Today, starting a job search means looking far beyond a list of tasks. The way we work has changed dramatically in recent years. Hybrid and remote working are now part of everyday language, and expectations.

What's even more transformative is the rise of tools that simply didn't exist a decade ago. Artificial intelligence platforms such as ChatGPT can help you to explore career options, refine your CV, draft powerful applications, practise interview answers, and even suggest new career paths based on your skills.

Remember though - AI is a **support tool**, not a substitute for **self-reflection**.
Just like the young man in this story, you'll still need to do the inner work. Clarity doesn't come from technology—it comes from **you**.

INTRODUCTION

This book is part of the **REVEAL system**—a complete, strategic approach to career advancement in today's competitive and AI-influenced job market. REVEAL equips you with everything you need to uncover your potential, stand out from the crowd, and succeed in your job search with confidence and clarity.

Here, we're focusing on just one step of that system: the **ELITE framework**, which guides you through the job application process, with a particular focus on writing a powerful CV.

Other books in the REVEAL series focus on related essentials such as cover letters and interview preparation. Each resource is designed to help you master a key milestone on your path to career success.

Now, let's begin.

The dictionary will tell you that a CV is a historical record of your skills, qualifications, and employment. The term *Curriculum Vitae* literally translates as "the course of one's life."

All well and good, but a CV is so much more than a summary of your experience. It's a business proposal. It's a marketing document. And it's your opportunity to communicate your value to someone who knows absolutely nothing about you. Your potential employer has never met you, so your CV needs to do the heavy lifting and make an immediate impact.

There's a striking graphic on *Business Insider* (Resume Heat Map - Business Insider) that reveals exactly where a recruiter's eyes go when they first scan a CV, and it's quite literally an eye-opener.

Picture this: someone in HR, sifting through hundreds of applications, spending mere seconds on each one. Their gaze lands first on your personal details, then your profile, your most recent role (if you've had one), and your highest academic qualification. And then—they stop. That's it. If those sections don't grab their attention, the rest may never even be seen.

And that's assuming your CV even makes it that far.

Many larger organizations and businesses now use Applicant Tracking Systems (ATS) - automated software that scans CVs and filters them before a human ever sees them. These systems look for specific keywords, job titles, and formatting cues. If your CV isn't structured clearly or doesn't reflect the language of the job description, it may be rejected automatically.

So, knowing that you might only have the time it takes to read this sentence to convince someone you're worth a second look, and that your CV could influence the course of your entire career, how much time would you spend preparing it? A couple of hours? A couple of days? And if just a couple of hours seems too much like hard work, you must ask yourself this: How important is this job to you?

You are unique, as is your future employer. That's why every application must be tailored to the specific role. No two jobs are exactly alike, and no two CVs should be either.

This book will walk you through how to do that, step-by-step, using the **ELITE framework**:

- **Examine** what you want
- **Learn** where to find the right opportunities
- **Itemize** your value
- **Tell** your story with clarity
- **Enhance** your message and make it shine

Now let's get started, because the right opportunity won't wait forever.

AI Tip

If writing your CV feels overwhelming, consider using AI tools to support the process—but not replace it.

Try asking ChatGPT:
"Here is a list of my past experience and strengths. Can you help me draft a short personal profile for my CV?"

Use the response as a springboard and then fine-tune it until it sounds like *you*.
AI can help you get started—but it's your personality, clarity, and authenticity that will make your CV stand out.

How to use this book

You will find that each of the activities in this book form building blocks that are going to help you create a CV or job application that gets you noticed for the right reasons.

Get yourself a notebook or journal and a pen or pencil to make notes because nothing is set in stone, and you may find yourself wanting to go back and make changes to your work.

Whilst the step-by-step process is easy to follow, be honest with yourself about what you want and what you're good at. Take time to reflect, and if you're unsure about what to do next, instead of applying logic to your decisions, notice how you *feel* about your ideas. You may be surprised by some of the insights you have.

AI Tip:

As you go through the exercises, you may want to test your answers using a tool such as ChatGPT, for example:
"Can you help me turn this into a short professional summary?"
"Which kind of roles match this list of skills and interests?"
"What are some companies that align with these values?"

Let AI act as your assistant, *but never let it decide for you.* The strongest applications come from those who have taken time to reflect.

STEP ONE. EXAMINE
THE CAREER COMPASS

"Begin with the end in mind" – Stephen Covey

I know that you can be whoever you want to be. Research suggests that up to 95% of our personality and behaviour is shaped by conditioning, from parents, teachers, media, and society.[1] But that doesn't mean it's who you truly are. My goal is to help you rediscover the real you - the one beneath all the layers, with clarity, confidence, and choice.

So - do you believe in yourself?

If you knew that success was guaranteed, what would you do?

If you didn't have to worry about what your family thought or deal with the consequences of your choice, which career would you choose?

A lot of people believe that they are under pressure to find a job purely for the sake of being able to pay the bills. An even greater number of people don't bother to apply for a job that they really want because they have convinced themselves that they aren't clever enough or that competition is too tough.

Fair enough.

But that is no excuse to send the same CV off to five or even 50 companies and then wonder why you aren't being invited for an interview. Consider carefully what is important to you and decide what you want, because if you don't know, you could have a hard time finding it.

If you love being around other people, if you love food, working in a friendly environment and have the patience to do repetitive work with regular hours, you might be happiest working in a bakery; you are never going to be happy working as a train driver.

By the same token, if you like working outside in the fresh air and enjoy some solitude, you are going to be better off working on a farm or as a landscape architect as opposed to having a 9 to 5 office job in a building with hundreds of other people.

EXERCISE 1

Start off by writing a list of everything you love to do. Think back to when you were a child.
- Did you love to dance, or read books, or play in the garden?
- What was it about those activities that made them fun?
- What do you enjoy doing now?
- What do other people tell you you're good at, even if it seems so easy to you that it doesn't seem important?

EXERCISE 2

Now write down EVERYTHING that your dream job would include. Get into as much detail as you possibly can to the extent that you can imagine yourself already doing work that you love. Here are some questions to answer to start you off:

- Will you work with a large or a small company?
- Private or public sector?
- What does the company do?
- What sort of people work there?
- What do you want to do there – are you working in a support or management role?
- What do you love doing?
- What policies does the company have in place to support its staff? The environment?
- What are your working hours?
- How much do you want to earn (don't sell yourself short but be realistic)?
- What are the benefits, such as holidays, or private health insurance?
- What does your office or working space look like?
- What will you place on your desk?
- Which types of conversations are you having?
- What can you see outside of your office window?
- Are you working in an office or from your kitchen table?
- Do you drive, walk or take public transport to your place of work?

The list can be as long or as short as you would like it to be, but take time to identify every aspect of what is important to you about a job, and write it down.

BRAINSTORM and DARE TO DREAM because it's free !

-

> **AI Tip**
> Use AI to explore ideas, not decide for you.
> Once you have completed your list, you could try asking an AI tool such as ChatGPT:
> *"Here's my dream job description. Which types of roles or industries might match?"*
> *"Can you help me create a list of European-based companies that align with these values?"*
> *"Which keywords should I search for based on this vision?"*
> Use this to expand your awareness, not to skip the thinking part. Your clarity still comes from within.

Room for compromise?

We generally tend to scour job vacancy notices and look at those that *sort of fit* what it is we're looking for. Being laser-focused not only on what you want to do, but also which type of environment you would like to work in and the type of people you feel most comfortable working with is going to save you a lot of time and heartache.

If you find yourself in a job that you don't love, where you don't feel appreciated and you're not using your skills, the chances are that you will eventually become miserable, and I have never met anyone who wants to be miserable all the time.

You may not believe that you can have everything that you want. So, could you compromise on your journey time or working hours? Or is spending time with your family in the evenings an important part of your day that you are not willing to give up?

You may find that by the end of this activity that you have changed your mind about something, and that's fine. Just be aware of how you feel about each of your choices and follow your instincts.

EXERCISE 3

Your two lists from Exercises 1 and 2 will already have given you a better idea of the direction you want to go in. You now need to put your list in order of priority so that when you start your job search you know where areas of potential compromise might be (or not).

Start off by comparing the first two items on your list (which will be much longer than the one here). Which of those two are more important to you? Put a cross or a tick next to the item that you choose.

In this example I have decided that it would be more important to earn € 2000 per month than to work for a small company. Having to decide between boxes one and three, my choice would be box three, to work 30 hours per month. Then I compare box one with box four, box one with box five, box one with box six, and so on.

I want to work for a small company	
I want to earn € 2000 per month	X
I want to work 30 hours per month	X
I love talking to people	
I love cooking and food	
I want to travel a maximum of 15 minutes to work	
I want private health insurance	
I love spending time outside	

Then you start again by comparing box two with box three, box two with box four, box two with box five ... then move to box three and compare it with box four, box three with box five ... then move to box four and compare it with box five ... keep going until you have worked your way through the entire list, always marking the statement that is more important.

My example now looks like this:

1.	I want to work for a small company	
2.	I want to earn EUR 2000 per month	x x x x
3.	I want to work 30 hours per month	x x x x
4.	I love talking to people	x x x x x x
5.	I love cooking and food	x x x x x x x
6.	I want to travel a maximum of 15 minutes to work	x
7.	I want private health insurance	x x x x
8.	I love spending time outside	xx

What I have learned from this is that although I thought that working for a small company was quite important to me, in comparison to the other things I want, it has become completely irrelevant. I have also learned that I would probably be happy to have a longer journey to work if the other things I wanted were in place.

Now it's your turn. Draw a table in your notebook and start making your choices.

AI Tip

Turning Priorities into Search Filters

Once you have completed your priorities, you can ask an AI tool to help you write job board filters or search phrases based on what matters most. For example:

"Write a Boolean search for jobs in London with flexible hours and values-driven Organizations."

"Based on these priorities, which job titles or sectors should I search for on LinkedIn?"

This is how you make technology work for your clarity—not the other way around.

STEP TWO. LEARN
WHERE SHOULD YOU LOOK FOR YOUR JOB?

"If opportunity doesn't knock, build a door." – Milton Berle

When we think about looking for a job, the first thing that most of us do is to check out online job portals, newspapers or magazines, or visit our local job centre. There's nothing wrong with any of these, but you need to be aware that the chances of finding a job using only these methods are quite slim.

According to career development professionals, only around 20 to 30 per cent of jobs are ever advertised publicly.

The vast majority of opportunities - the other 70 to 80 per cent - are found through what is known as the hidden job market. This includes jobs that are:

- Given to internal candidates
- Shared through networks and referrals
- Filled by people who approached the company directly

This means that the way you look for work needs to include both *formal* and *informal* strategies.

If you focus only on job advertisements, you might be missing out on the roles that never get posted at all.

AI Tip
Use AI to build a smarter search strategy
Try asking:
"Can you suggest five lesser-known places or websites where roles in [your industry] are advertised in the UK?"
"Which strategies do people use to tap into the hidden job market in my field?"
AI can act as a brainstorming partner to help you go beyond the usual job boards.

Informal job search strategies

- Speak to your friends and family. Let them know what you're looking for.
- Ask people to keep their eyes and ears open for you.
- Get in touch with former colleagues.

It can feel scary to reach out like this, but many jobs are filled because someone made a positive impression at the right time.

EXERCISE 5

Write down a list of at least **five people** you could contact. These might include:
- People you have worked with in the past
- Friends or neighbours in your area
- Former managers or supervisors
- Mentors, tutors or teachers
- People you know through volunteering or social groups

Remember that you are not asking them for favours – you are asking if they have heard of any opportunities, or if they know of someone who can point you in the right direction.

Formal job search strategies

These include:
- Job search portals (Indeed, LinkedIn Jobs, Civil Service, Charity Job)
- Local and regional newspapers or online magazines
- Professional associations
- Recruitment agencies and consultants

You can also sign up for alerts so that you are notified of new positions matching your keywords.

Remember too that it can be very useful to put your job title and location into your internet search engine and go through the first couple of pages of results.

AI Tip

Customise your job alerts using AI

You can ask your AI to help you optimise your search. For example:

"Can you help me to write a Boolean search string for policy advisor roles in NGOs, based in [COUNTRY] posted in the last 14 days?"

"Based on my experience and interests, which keywords should I use to get the best job alerts on LinkedIn?"

These search refinements can save you time and will make sure that you are only seeing relevant, recent opportunities.

Using LinkedIn and social media

LinkedIn is an essential platform for job seekers. It's not just for networking, it's also where many recruiters search for candidates directly, and in our age of technology, if you do not have a so-called *online footprint*, you may stand out for the wrong reasons.

Make sure:
- Your profile is up to date
- Your photo is professional
- Your headline reflects what you're looking for
- Your 'About' section includes key skills, achievements and values
- You are actively connecting with people and engaging with content

You can also follow companies you're interested in and comment on their posts to stay visible.

AI Tip

Optimise your LinkedIn profile with AI (then personalise it)

Do you need help refining your headline or 'About' section? Try asking AI:

"Can you help me write a strong LinkedIn headline for someone looking for a role in [insert field]?"

"Can you improve this LinkedIn summary to make it confident, clear and values-based?"

AI can help you structure your message, but your voice and values must still shine through.

EXERCISE 6

- If you are not already on LinkedIn, create a profile today. If you are, review it using the checklist above.
- What can you improve or update?
- Make a short action list and schedule 15–30 minutes a week to maintain your profile and activity.

STEP THREE - ITEMIZE
WHY SHOULD AN EMPLOYER CHOOSE TO INTERVIEW YOU?

"What lies before us and what lies behind us are very little compared to what lies within us" – Ralph Waldo Emerson

As quickly as technology advances, so our attention spans decrease, and you have just a few seconds to grab the attention of a human and convince them to put your application onto the pile for a closer look.

When it comes to marketing or branding yourself, I like to use the example of washing products so please bear with me. Think back to the last time you saw an advertisement for some washing powder. Did an actor stand there with the product in their hands, read the chemical contents out loud and say 'this washes well, please buy it'? Probably not.

Instead you will have seen smiling faces, the sun shining, happy children, bright colours, clean washing, do you see where I'm going with this? It's not enough to tell your potential employer about what you can do, you must be able to paint a picture for them about how brilliant you are so that they can already imagine you standing (or sitting) in front of them.

So moving from washing powder to you, how will you position yourself so that a hiring manager instantly sees your value? In other words, what is your personal brand, and how are you going to showcase it?

When answering these questions you may be tempted to put yourself into a 'box' and call yourself a secretary or a solicitor. But that isn't who you are. They are merely titles and don't mean much on paper, especially if you are being compared with others who have a similar title. You want the person reading your CV to *feel* how it might be to work with you.
Here's another question. How does your definition of 'qualified' differ from that of your

potential employer? How many times have you said yourself or heard others say that someone was not qualified?

You may be at the point where you have decided that your work experience and academic qualifications just about meet the requirements of the job vacancy, but it is equally important that you help your potential employer to understand who you are.

Can you can be trusted? Are you detail oriented? Do you work well in a team, or do you prefer working on your own initiative? Do you like a routine or do you get bored easily? How do you handle disagreements at work? How good are you at persuading others? How would you deal with a mistake that you made? How do you deal with deadlines and stress? How important is it to you to follow the 'policies and rules' of the company?

Which specific examples can you give for all of these qualities and skills?

None of these are likely to be easy questions to address, and they will take some time to answer. You are unique, and if you want to market yourself successfully then you absolutely must know *what you do well* before you start writing your CV.

Remember that you have just seconds to convince someone to put your application onto the 'for interview' pile. By including *you*, the human being, in your CV, you are going to stand out from the other 95 per cent of applicants who have simply copied and pasted a list of their previous tasks and responsibilities. Get it all out of your brain and onto paper.

EXERCISE 7
How would you describe yourself to others? If you get stuck, how would a colleague or friend describe you?

AI Tip
Use AI to test your messaging (only after reflection)
Once you've written a short description of your personal brand, you can test it by asking: *"Can you help me phrase this in a way that sounds confident and professional, but still authentic?"*
Use what AI gives you as inspiration, never as a substitute for your own voice.

STEP FOUR - TELL
GATHERING THE FACTS

"Get your facts first, then you can distort them as you please." – Mark Twain

There seems to be a general rule that a CV should not be longer than two pages, but it will always depend upon the job that you are applying for, and the level of detail that the employer has asked you to provide. At the other end of the spectrum, many online application forms can be surprisingly long, sometimes stretching to close to 20 pages.

Before you start twisting yourself into knots about application length though, take some time to copy all your key information into a Word document. In the long term this master file will save you time, reduce stress, and serve as the foundation for every application you complete moving forward.

This type of advance preparation will also mean that you won't lose your data if the online system goes down before you've managed to save everything.

EXERCISE 8
Create a 'word' or similar document and add your answers for all of the following.

Your name
A great way to start your CV is to put your name at the top, in capital, bold letters, followed by basic contact details.

Telephone number

Where can you be contacted most easily? If you are applying internationally, can a potential employer contact you via WhatsApp?

Providing a landline number can be risky:

1. If you share a home with young children or elderly relatives, a call from a potential employer might be answered in a way that doesn't create the best first impression.
2. Listing your current work telephone number could backfire if a colleague picks up the telephone when you're not at your desk, especially if your job search is confidential (which it should be)

Email address

Consider setting up an email address specifically for your job search. This will help you to keep track of where you have sent applications to and when, instead of having to search through other personal correspondence.

Use something relevant such as your full name, or the first initial of your first name followed by your family name, or a similar format. Take care too with numbers as it is difficult to tell the difference between the letter 'l', and the number '1' – make sure that the email address is easy to read.

The majority of companies have an email/internet policy that will include a rule about using it for official purposes only, and using your work email address (if you are currently employed) for job applications could be problematic because if there were justification to do so, your employer could have access to your email account, and if you have not told anyone about your job search, you could find yourself leaving your job earlier than anticipated. This would of course be an extreme case, but keep it in mind.

Date of birth

According to EU legislation an employer is not allowed to ask for your date of birth during the application process, unless it can be proved that it is relevant to the work in question. You will be aware however that the employer will be able to guess your approximate age from the information you provide about your education, and many companies and organizations with application forms still ask you to provide those details.

Marital status and dependents

Again, this is not relevant to your ability to do a job, and most people leave it off a CV. That said, some international organizations may ask for your marital status if benefits for dependents - such as housing, education, or relocation support - are a part of the employment package.

Your Profile: How are you going to describe yourself?

Your CV profile is prime real estate and it's often the very first thing that a recruiter sees. It may well be the only part they read before deciding whether to keep going. You cannot assume that they will start with your application or cover letter, so your profile needs to do the heavy lifting. It's your chance to introduce who you are, not just what you do, to showcase your values, your energy, and the unique perspective you bring. In a few short lines, you can make a human connection and capture their attention before they move on to the next CV.

That said, please remember that this kind of profile is only relevant when you're creating and submitting your own CV. If you're completing an online application form, there's often little or no space for a personal profile at the top. In such cases you'll need to shift your focus to the cover letter, where you can bring your personality, values, and motivation to life.

Whilst the CV in a structured form may limit how much of *you* can shine through, your cover letter becomes the place to make that all-important first impression.

Career history

List the names and addresses of previous employers (if applicable), and your dates of employment in reverse chronological order (ie.,include the most recent first). Describe your key duties and responsibilities (we are going to look at how you present that information a little later).

Which examples can you use to describe your activities? Find examples of what you did well, how your input made a difference (ask yourself the question 'so what?'), and write down everything you can think of that is going to help paint your picture.

Education

List the details of university or college courses including the grade achieved, and your dates of study. Include the most recent first.

Professional membership

If you are in the medical profession you may belong to the Medical Council, or if you work in finance you may belong to one of the Chartered Institutes.

Training and development

Make a list of all the courses you have studied which were not a part of your formal education for example career coaching, or IT packages, or even training with the Red Cross as a volunteer.

Publications

These will usually be more relevant to positions requiring very specific qualifications in the medical, legal or educational sectors.

Voluntary work

Have you taken part in any activities to support others?

Other information

Most employers will want to know whether you have a valid driving licence. Also include information about any languages you speak, in addition to your mother tongue. As for hobbies, what impression are you trying to create?

For example if you say that you love reading and fishing but are applying for a job as a sales person, your CV could end up in the 'no' pile because you have given the impression that you prefer to be on your own enjoying some peace and quiet.

If you are invited for interview and have included an unusual or exotic hobby, be prepared to talk about it, because if one of the people interviewing you asks you where your favourite site for deep-sea diving is, and the closest you have been to water in recent years is your shower, you could be in trouble!

Referees

Including the details of your referees on your CV will take up a lot of precious space. If a company has decided that it really likes you and wants to offer you the job, it is generally assumed that they will ask to provide references, so leave those details off your CV and provide them only if asked.

That said, make sure that you know who you would like to ask in advance (you must ask permission from the person you wish to use as a referee).

So who could you ask? Are they familiar with your work experience, academic qualifications and/or character? Most employers will ask for three referees, but you might want to ask four or five people when you start your job search so that you can select those that can provide information that is relevant for the job in question. Put their names and contact details in your job search file/journal.

And finally - and this really is going to be the most important change you make to your CV or application - get ready to dig deeper into everything you've written. This will take time, and the time that you take is going to help you stand out from all the other candidates.

For every sentence you have included, ask yourself: "So what?"
Then immediately answer with: "So that..."
- Why was that task or achievement important?
- Who benefitted from it?
- What changed as a result?
- What did it help solve, improve, or deliver?

This simple but powerful shift helps you move from just listing responsibilities to clearly communicating your impact. It takes your CV from generic to memorable. It shows that you understand your role in a wider context and that you have thought about how your work contributes to something meaningful.

Yes, this exercise takes time. Yes, it may feel uncomfortable at first.

But the results will be what sets your application apart from the rest. Firstly, you will have triggered a pattern interrupt of the brain of the person reading (because it isn't a boring list) and secondly you will have demonstrated that you have carefully considered what the hiring manager is looking for.

Keep going until you understand what your real contribution was to each of your previous jobs, because when you can see it, so can the employer. And that can be the difference between being overlooked and being invited to interview.

AI Tip

Use it to practise your "so what → so that" thinking

If you're stuck, try giving AI a task that you've listed and ask:

"Help me turn this task into a result-driven statement by answering 'so what?' and 'so that...'"

For example:

"I organised weekly team meetings."

becomes

"I organised weekly team meetings so that everyone was aligned with their priorities, which helped us reduce missed deadlines by 30%."

Then tweak it until it feels real and honest for you.

In summary what you will have created is a very basic template for a chronological CV, set out again below (and you can find a link to download a word template on my website at the end of this book)

NAME
Address:
Telephone:
Email:
Date of birth (optional):

Example of a Profile:

Describe yourself in terms of the job for which you are applying ie., if you are applying for a job as a project officer but much of your experience has been in a support role: *A well-organized administrator who has contributed to and/or managed a number of successful projects in the field of education/public administration reform.* Include your key skills and expertise, not only the technical qualifications but also your 'soft' skills

CAREER HISTORY

Most recent job title
Organization
Dates
Brief description of the company
Key achievements
Do *not* copy/paste your job description. Select relevant skills and experience to the position for which you are applying.

QUALIFICATIONS

Higher academic qualifications should be listed first

TRAINING

Include information that is *relevant* for each application.

ADDITIONAL INFORMATION

Voluntary work, driving license, language skills etc.

HOBBIES (if you want to)

Structuring Your CV to Get Noticed

You have already gathered the facts, written down key achievements, and thought carefully about your strengths. Now it's time to structure your CV in a way that helps it stand out, whether it's being read by a human or scanned by an algorithm.

This section is worth reading through several times.

Understanding How Employers Think

Most job descriptions will look something like this (although some will be longer and more specific):

Example:

Tasks and responsibilities

- Provides clerical and administrative support to the team
- Deals with telephone and email enquiries
- Manages the departmental budget
- Coordinates departmental projects
- Manages the diary of the Director

Required qualifications

- College Diploma
- Proven ability to manage projects
- Minimum of two years' work experience
- Excellent written and spoken communication skills in English

Competences
- Teamwork
- Analytical skills
- Communication skills

The employer includes this list for a reason. It tells you what they value, and who they're looking for. Your job is to match your experience and qualities to their needs.

Remember, the person reviewing your CV probably helped write the job description and they will be scanning your application with that list in mind. You need to grab their attention fast.

Three Ways to Make Your CV Stand Out

1. Mirror the keywords in the job description
Use the exact phrases from the job description. For example, if it mentions 'telephone and email enquiries,' include that exact wording in your CV. Do not assume that a similar phrase will be enough.

This is especially important when applying to large organizations that use Applicant Tracking Systems (ATS). These systems scan CVs for specific keywords before a human even sees them. If those keywords are missing, your application may be rejected automatically.

AI Tip
Use AI to find the right keywords
Upload the job description into ChatGPT and ask:
"What are the top 10 keywords or phrases I should reflect in my CV for this role?"
This can help ensure you're including the terms that matter most.

---

2. Match priorities
Job descriptions usually list responsibilities in order of importance. You should do the same in your CV.

Let's say your current job involves diary management and team support. If the employer puts 'administrative support' first and 'diary management' last, emphasise the team support part of your role, even if you spend more time on the diary. This helps the employer immediately see that you can do what they care about most.

3. Describe the person they're looking for

Put yourself in the employer's shoes: what kind of person would you hire for the role?

One client I worked with was applying for a role related to mediation. They originally described themselves as "enthusiastic." But after reflecting on what a good mediator looks like, they changed their wording to "diplomatic," "discreet," and "sincere." These characteristics made a much stronger impression.

Read the vacancy text again, and again. Which values or personality traits are implied? What kind of person would thrive in that setting?

Again, this work takes time, but it pays off when you get that call to come in for interview. Onwards!

EXERCISE 9

Keep a note of all the keywords that come up in job descriptions. Keep them handy as you write your CV and application.

Standing Out from the Crowd

Here are two examples that show how to move from flat, generic statements to something more memorable. Do you remember the *"so what, so that"* exercise?

Example 1

Boring: Good communicator and works well in teams.
Better: Led a team of eight to create and deliver a training plan that helped increase sales.

Example 2

Boring: Advised the Director of HR.
Better: Recommended changes to the HR process that were approved and cut the annual budget.

The first sentences give plain facts - they tell you *what* was done. The second ones show *how well* it was done and give a sense of the impact.

AI Tip

Turn general statements into achievements.

Try: *"Here's a list of things I've done at work. Can you rewrite them to show the result of each one?"*

Use the suggestions as a starting point, then edit to reflect your voice and truth.

Connect Your CV to the Organization

The best CVs are tailored not only to the job, but to the organization itself.

What does their website say about them? What tone do they use in their communications? Which values do they promote?

If you are genuinely excited about joining their team, your CV should show that. Align your tone and values with theirs while staying true to yourself.

AI Tip

Speed up your company research

Ask:

"Summarise the mission, values, and tone of voice on [Company Name]'s website."

Or: *"What does this company focus on in its public messaging?"*

Let AI spot themes, but you decide what matters most.

The Role of the Profile

Some CV templates include a professional profile at the top in the form of a short paragraph that highlights who you are and what you're about. When well written it can quickly capture attention and encourage the recruiter to keep reading.

This only applies if you're structuring your own CV however because online application forms do not usually leave room for this kind of summary, so you'll need to share that information in your cover letter instead.

If you do include a profile, make sure that it reflects your personality, values, and working style, not just your job title.

Example:

"In my capacity as a manager, throughout my working experience in a multi-national environment, my excellent inter-personal skills have contributed to the successful implementation of three training projects which supported staff to meet their professional objectives. In addition to my university studies I have trained as a Project Management Professional (PMP) and I enjoy working with teams who are goal-oriented and committed to producing results."

In just a few lines, this tells the employer that the candidate is a skilled communicator, an experienced team leader, and someone who finishes what they start.

AI Tip

Try:

"Can you help me refine this summary so it sounds confident, authentic, and clear—without making it generic?"

Or if you're unsure where to begin:

"Here are five things I'm proud of in my work. Can you help me turn this into a short professional summary?"

Final Tips

Sometimes application forms ask you to list your skills and strengths and/or achievements separately. But a list on its own won't say much. You will need examples to show how you use those strengths in real life. So, take a fresh look at your work experience section. Go line by line and ask: *"Have I shown the best of what I can do here?"*

And remember:
- What picture are you painting?
- What are you proud of?
- What do you do really well?
- What do others say your strengths are?

It might take time to find the right words, but once you have crafted your profile and shaped your CV, all future applications will be faster and easier to adapt to the job vacancy in question.

STEP FIVE - ENHANCE
BRINGING IT ALL TOGETHER

**"Do your little bit of good where you are;
it's those little bits of good put together that overwhelm the world."
– Desmond Tutu**

You have almost finished …

Did you complete the exercise to create a word document that contained your entire professional history, even if it meant that your document was several pages long?

Now it's time to go into the final details.

The length of your CV will depend upon the seniority of the position in question and what the employer has asked you to provide. Your goal should always be to provide something that is concise and relevant, and which helps the person reading to get a feel for who you are.

If you followed the recommendations in 'Step Four – TELL', you will already have the order of items to include on your CV. There are some differences between European and North American formats in that the order of work experience and education is switched around. Depending upon where you live you will easily be able to find out which is appropriate.

If you are putting your information into a pre-formatted application form, you will have instructions about what to put where.

> **AI Tip**
> Use AI to help you summarise and tailor your CV
> If your CV is too long, paste in a section and ask:
> *"Can you help me shorten this experience to 2–3 bullet points that focus on achievements relevant to [insert job title]?"*
> AI won't decide for you, but it can help with clarity, focus, and trimming without losing the message.

Checklist:

Your CV should be easy to read, with clear headings and adequate spacing between sections.

- Use an 'easy to read' font, such as 'Times New Roman' or 'Calibri'.

- Use a single colour, preferably black.

- Refrain from inserting lines and boxes to split up the information on your CV. Lines and boxes can irritate the eyes and you are better off writing section titles in capital letters or bold text.

- If necessary use bullet points formatted as dashes (the traditional round bullet points take up too much space) to describe your work experience, and if you are writing a CV as opposed to an application form I would suggest that you include a maximum of five *relevant* bullet points for each position. You may also like to consider writing a brief narrative/summary for each job.

- Decide which parts of your work experience match the requirements of the job in question. If you are running out of space consider including just one or two bullet points (or a short summary) for previous jobs that do not fully match the requirements of the current vacancy.

- Spell check what you have written. Print off your CV and ask someone else to look at it. Although I am a staunch supporter of protecting the environment, most printing paper these days is from trees farmed specifically for office use, and you can always put your draft papers back into the recycling box when you know you have found all the changes that need to be made.

-

Final suggestions:

1. Read the job application carefully and follow submission instructions to the letter. If the company or organization is asking for a CV, send a CV. *Do not* use the application form of another employer.

2. Do not send a photograph unless specifically asked to do so. If you happen to be wearing a pink shirt in your photograph and the person looking at your CV thinks that pink is a horrible colour, you could be putting yourself at a disadvantage.

3. If you are asked to provide a cover letter, do so. Pick out three strengths/skills that you believe are key for the position and describe how they will help your new employer in detail. If you are asked to provide a letter of motivation, remember to tell the employer WHY you want the position.

4. Give your CV document your name. Include your name and the name of the vacancy at the bottom of each page (in the footer). This will make it much easier for HR staff to identify your details when going through hundreds of other applications.

5. When sending your CV by email, include the vacancy notice number/title in the subject bar, and double check that you have attached your CV!

6. If you are sending a hard copy application, use an A4 envelope (do not fold your application), and use a paper clip to keep the papers together. If you were the person in HR with the task of having to photocopy lots of CVs, you would not want to be spending time removing fiddly staples.

AI Tip

Once you have finalised your CV, upload it into your AI and ask:

"Can you review this for consistency in formatting, tone, and spacing?"

Or:

"Can you flag anything in this CV that might be hard to read or visually inconsistent?"

It's not a replacement for a trusted human reviewer, but it's a very useful second pass before you print or submit.

RESULT!

Congratulations!

You now have the basis of a fantastic CV, a document that will help employers understand how fabulous you really are, and which will stand out from the other applications, increasing your chances of an interview.

Of course some changes will still have to be made depending upon the job that you are applying to – remember to pick out and include key words relevant to the vacancy - but the majority of the hard work is behind you.

Before you go ...
There are no secrets on the internet, so take a moment to look at your social media profiles as if you were a stranger. What impression do you get?

Do any of your photos, posts, or jokes need to be removed? Have your views changed over time, so that older posts no longer reflect who you are today?

Would you feel comfortable seeing one of your posts on the front page of a newspaper?

Take a moment to 'Google' yourself and review the search results—because if an employer is interested, there's every chance they will do the same.

If you find something you'd rather not see there, you can request removal through Google.

Change your profile picture on social media platforms if needed and use your social networks to present the professional image you want employers to see.

AI Tip

Do you want to make sure your online presence reflects the best version of you? Try asking AI:

"Can you help me write a short, professional LinkedIn summary that reflects my strengths in [insert industry/role]?"

Or:

"What kind of tone or impression does my online profile give? How could I improve it for potential employers?"

AI can help you craft a confident, consistent image across platforms, but only you can decide what feels true.

That's it! Please do come and connect with me either via email, LinkedIn or YouTube - you'll find all the links at the end of the book - and I wish you every success in finding the job of your dreams.

"You have brains in your head, you have feet in your shoes, you can steer yourself in any direction you choose." Dr Seuss

QUESTIONS AND ANSWERS

Here are some of the questions that I am asked, together with my answers.

Question: There are gaps in my CV because I was unemployed. What should I write?
Answer: This is one of those million-dollar questions. If you were unemployed due to redundancy, restructuring, or a merger, it's fine to include that information. But you must also show how you used your time.

you might explain that you have been focusing on professional development, researching the job market, or networking. Did you do any volunteering or community work? If not, and if the gap is relatively short, you may also choose to simply leave it blank.

Question: I was ill for a long time so wasn't working. Should I include that on my CV?
Answer: Another tough one. But unless your illness will affect your ability to do the job, there is no need to provide details.

Question: Should I include the reason for wanting to leave my job?
Answer: If you are leaving your job voluntarily, you'll hopefully have a good reason. But keep in mind - 'I didn't get on with my boss' or 'I want a pay rise' are not things a potential employer wants to read. Put yourself in the shoes of the hiring manager: which reasons would you find acceptable?

Question: Should I tell the truth?
Answer: ALWAYS!

Question: What should I write about if I don't have any work experience because I'm only just leaving school/college/university?
Answer: Focus on how quick you are to learn and what your strengths are. Give specific examples of how you take initiative and get things done. Even if you haven't yet been employed, your application must still show the employer how they will benefit from having you on the team. Paint that picture, just like anyone else would.

AI Tip

If you're unsure how to phrase a sensitive issue—like a career break, redundancy, or lack of experience—you can ask:

"Can you help me explain this career gap in a way that feels honest, professional, and positive?"

Or:

"Here's how I want to explain leaving my job. Can you help me rephrase this so it sounds constructive?"

AI can help you express things clearly and confidently—but you decide what's true and appropriate to share.

ADDITIONAL READING AND USEFUL LINKS

Covey, S. (2004) "The 7 Habits of Highly Effective People: Powerful Lessons in Personal Change"

Hendricks, G. PhD (2009) "The Big Leap: Conquer Your Hidden Fear and Take Life to the Next Level"

Letherbarrow, G (2017) "Interviews and Videos: Present Like a Pro and Nail That Job!'

Download a simple CV Template **HERE**
Or visit www.feelgoodcoachingandconsulting.com/free-resources

ABOUT THE AUTHOR

Gwyneth is an Award-Winning Coach and People Strategist who has helped thousands of professionals enhance their presence, position themselves for leadership, and unlock new opportunities for growth and success.

Born in England, she spent over 20 years working with international organizations across Europe and the Balkans, leading, developing, and sometimes drawing down multicultural teams. These hands-on experiences gave her deep insight into the unique challenges and remarkable opportunities that cross-cultural collaboration presents.

With a background in management, marketing, and human resources, Gwyneth is passionate about the power of **emotional intelligence**—both for building strong working relationships and advancing professional development. Whether supporting individuals to navigate their next career move or working with organizations to improve team cohesion, she blends strategic thinking with practical, people-focused solutions.

Her work now includes **cutting-edge AI integration**, allowing her to offer smarter, faster support to clients navigating complex workplace dynamics—particularly in culturally diverse environments where clarity, trust, and alignment are essential. By balancing emerging technologies with a human-centred approach, Gwyneth ensures that her clients are prepared for the future of work without losing the human connection that drives performance.

Today, Gwyneth supports two main groups:
1. **Leaders and senior managers of cross-cultural teams**, helping them tackle miscommunication, cultural misunderstandings, and low engagement that often hinder growth.
2. **Professionals at a career crossroads**, whether seeking a promotion, navigating job transitions, or re-entering the workforce with renewed confidence and clarity.

Her signature framework, the **Cross-Cultural COHESION Code**, is a practical, proven system that combines emotional intelligence strategies with AI-driven tools to build trust, empathy, and performance across diverse teams. Meanwhile, her **VIP Career Breakthrough** and **REVEAL** programmes empower individuals to take control of their careers, develop next-level leadership presence, and stand out in today's competitive job market.

This is not just coaching, it's a transformational journey delivered with clarity, precision, and measurable results.

If you're ready to create a high-performing team or elevate your own career with a tailored, intelligent strategy, Gwyneth is here to guide you.

To find out more about how Gwyneth can support you - and for details on her 1:1 coaching, workshops, and career development programmes - please get in touch.

Gwyneth Letherbarrow MBA
Award-Winning Coach │People Strategist │Author │Speaker
E: gwyneth@feelgoodcoachingandconsulting.com
WhatsApp: 0043 (0) 650 4111 744

YouTube: GwynethELYouTube
LinkedIn: /Gwyneth Letherbarrow

www.ingramcontent.com/pod-product-compliance
Lightning Source LLC
Chambersburg PA
CBHW081641220526
45468CB00009B/2521